The world of teens

Shaykh Muhammad Yahya Ibn Faruq

Second Edition

WHAT DOES ISLAM SAY?
Growing up
MUSIC-HALAL-OR-HARAAM
★ ★ Maturity
PARENTS
DATING
boyfriends/girlfriends
FACEBOOK
INTERNET
PUBERTY
MSN BUDDIES
FASHION ★ FRIENDS
TRIALS AND TRIBULATIONS

YOUTH ZONE

An Nasihah Publications

Every effort has been made to trace the copyright holders and to obtain their permission for the use of copyright material. The author and publishers will gladly receive information enabling them to rectify any error or omission in subsequent editions.

First Edition 2007
Second Edition 2011

An Nasihah Publications
P O BOX 7737
LEICESTER LE5 5XU. United Kingdom

Email : theworldof_teens@yahoo.com

©An Nasihah Publications

British Library Catalogue-in-Publication Data.

A CIP record for this book is available from the British Library.

ISBN 09548727 1 1

Distributors in the UK: Azhar Academy, London
www.azharacademy.com

Printed in Turkey by Imak Ofset Printers : isa@imakofset.com.tr

Design & Artwork by Rizwan Ahmed : riz160@yahoo.co.uk

Contents

Comments and Feedback

"I think that the World of Teens (1) was one of the best books I have read; because it was written in the way teenagers understand it best. There were also a lot of great examples which made it fun and easy to digest. I can't wait for part 2!" (Yusuf Patel. 16)

"...The World of Teens is probably the best fact-based book I've ever read. This is the first book I read in one go without getting bored..." (Muslim Sister. 19)

"....May Allah reward you for your efforts in writing this book. May Allah give me and other teenagers the strength to become good practising Muslims..." (Muslim Sister. 14)

"I read ur book and thoroughly enjoyed it. May Allah reward you for your loyal service to Deen." (Muslim Sister. 18)

"... I read your 'World of Teens Part One'. I really enjoyed it: it was really funny. Inshallah, if you keep on writing funny, interesting and mind blowing books, then inshallah you will become everyone's favourite author, because you are my favourite author (no joke)" (Harun Zaman, 14)

Acknowledgements

Special acknowledgements must go to: my respected parents and teachers who were always giving that extra word of encouragement to keep me going; my wife & son who were there to support me; my brothers and sisters for their continuous help despite my shortcomings; my English teacher Sir Siraj Lambat for his help once again; brother Abid Russell for the thorough editing and advice on many issues despite his busy schedule , Mufti Ebrahim Moosa for his assistance in setting the book; sister Amiza Nina for granting permission to use her poem A tribute to Mothers; brother Rizwan Ahmed for the beautiful design and artwork; all those young teens out there who sent their vital suggestions and feedback which compelled me to continue; my students who asked nearly every other day as to when part two was going to be released and all those who assisted with the publication of this book. May Allah grant them all and the whole Muslim Ummah a Hayatan Tayyibah (a happy peaceful life). Ameen.

Introduction

In the Name of Allah, the Most Beneficent, the Most Merciful. All Praises be to Allah ta'ala and peace and Salutations be upon the Best of Mankind: Muhammad.

Alhamdulillah, by the grace of My Lord the second part of this series is now in your hands. It is only Allah who made the first part a huge success, helping many teenagers change their lives and reform themselves into instrumental individuals. I pray to Allah that He makes part two also a means of guidance for all who read it. Ameen.

The purpose of this book is to assist the teen through the challenging years of his or her life, it is not a masail book explaining what is Halal and Haram. Whatever I have achieved it is through the dua and efforts of my teachers and family. May Allah lengthen their lives and grant them protection from all forms of illnesses. Ameen.

If you find any fault, then correct it I pray,
For no one is faultless except Allah
(Jalaaluddin Abd Ar Rahman As Sooyuti)

Muhammad Yahya Ibn Farouk
September 2007/ Ramadan 1428.

**WHEN YOU CAME INTO THE WORLD, SHE HELD YOU IN HER ARMS
YOU THANKED HER BY WAILING LIKE A BANSHEE...**

**WHEN YOU WERE 1 YEARS OLD, SHE FED YOU AND BATHED YOU
YOU THANKED HER BY CRYING ALL NIGHT...**

**WHEN YOU WERE 2 YEARS OLD, SHE TAUGHT YOU TO WALK
YOU THANKED HER BY RUNNING AWAY WHEN SHE CALLED...**

"My old man just can't keep it shut!"

"Nag! Nag! Nag! That's all he does all day!"

"Come on man, what do they know??? What faintest idea do they have of what's it like living in the modern ages? Huh! Just think everyone's like them."

Ever heard those words from your own mouth? Or maybe from others? Sadly, these are the usual sentences people use to describe their parents! Yes, dear brothers and sisters, it may seem that your parents are always nagging at you for whatever reason, but you have got to get this right:

if it weren't for our parents then we would never have existed, and if they hadn't looked after us then we would never have got to the age to read this.

Who was the one who stayed awake all night worrying

and caring for you? Who was it that sweated all day so you could have the best clothes?

Who was the one that forgave you a thousand and one times...?

It's true guys, we've really gotta think when we're at boiling points with our parents, that at the end of the day these people whom I'm about to explode upon are the actual cause of my existence in this world. What must they be going through at that very moment in time? When their once beautiful bouncing baby boy or girl starts threatening to bounce them?

Think!

Let's go a little into the future and catapult ourselves into their position:

Here we are, fifty years from today chilling oops sorry we won't be chilling at that age will we? Let's say breathing... having worked our guts out for our children, who've grown up now and seem to be fairly independent. Now, here I am sitting at home all day waiting for my ickle cuddly child to come and then I can listen to his day's activities and adventures...

Suddenly he/she comes barging in...

Flings the bag on the floor...

Storms upstairs...

And 'bang!' goes the bedroom door.

Let me see what's wrong... I climb the stairs gently...

Worrying and praying all the while as I reach the top...

And knock ever-so-softly on the door... thinking as to

what may have happened to my dear child: Has someone

hurt him? Did someone abuse her? Whatever the case

I shall most definitely help him...

**WHEN YOU WERE 3 YEARS OLD, SHE MADE ALL YOUR MEALS WITH LOVE
YOU THANKED HER BY TOSSING YOUR PLATE ON THE FLOOR...**

**WHEN YOU WERE 4 YEARS OLD, SHE GAVE YOU SOME CRAYONS
YOU THANKED HERE BY COLOURING THE DINING ROOM TABLE...**

**WHEN YOU WERE 5 YEARS OLD, SHE DRESSED YOU FOR THE HOLIDAYS
YOU THANKED HER BY PLOPPING INTO THE NEAREST PILE OF MUD...**

**WHEN YOU WERE 6 YEARS OLD, SHE WALKED YOU TO SCHOOL
YOU THANKED HER BY SCREAMING, "I'M NOT GOING!"**

No reply... I open the door slowly and say in the most

sympathetic tone I can summon: "Hey what's up

sweetheart?"

"Just shut your trap and mind your own business! You're too old to understand these kinda things!!!" What would be my reaction?

"Why that cheeky little blighter! I'll knock his/her lights out! Huh! Talking to me like that!"

Well lets think about a couple of reasons why my future self might not be up to it:

1. In fifty years time, I'll most likely have lost that speed and body strength. Kids can be very slippery for a creaking fifty year old.

2. Even if i did manage to maintain my strength due to some vitamins, then the embedded parental love just wouldn't allow me.

WHEN YOU WERE 7 YEARS OLD, SHE BOUGHT YOU A BALL.
YOU THANKED HER BY THROWING IT THROUGH THE NEXT-DOOR-NEIGHBOUR'S WINDOW...

WHEN YOU WERE 8 YEARS OLD, SHE HANDED YOU AN ICE CREAM.
YOU THANKED HER BY DRIPPING IT ALL OVER YOUR LAP...

WHEN YOU WERE 9 YEARS OLD, SHE PAID FOR PRIVATE LESSONS
YOU THANKED HER BY NEVER EVEN BOTHERING TO PAY ATTENTION...

WHEN YOU WERE 10 YEARS OLD, SHE DROVE YOU ALL DAY, FROM THE PLAYING FIELD TO ONE FRIEND'S PARTY AFTER ANOTHER
YOU THANKED HER BY JUMPING OUT AND NEVER LOOKING BACK...

WHEN YOU WERE 11 YEARS OLD, SHE TOOK YOU SHOPPING YOU THANKED HER BY DEMANDING TO BUY EVERYTHING YOU TOUCHED...

Bird Brain

Once there was an old father sitting in his garden, and alongside him his teenage son. The following is an account of what took place. Let us put ourselves this time in the teenager's position, how would we have reacted...?

Father: "My dear son!"

Son: "Yes dad!"

Father: "What is that on the tree?"

Son: "Dad it's a bird."

(10 minutes later...)

Father: "My dear son!"

Son: "Yes!"

Father: "What is that on the tree?"

Son: "I just told you it's a bird."

(10 minutes later...)

Father: "My dear son!"

Son: "What!!"

Father: "What is that on the tree?"

Son: "What are you playing at?? Huh? I told you once

IT'S A BIRD!!!

NOW DO U WANT ME TO SPELL IT OUT FOR YOU??

'B....   I....   R....   D.... !'

A minute later the father walks off to get something whilst the teenager mutters under his breath "Honestly! Old people just chat!"

Father returns with dusty leather bound diary and places it on the child's lap with a specific page opened...

Date: September 1993

Today my beloved 4 year old son asked me no less than 35 times

About a bird which was perched upon our tree as to what it was.

Each time I gave him the very same reply in exactly the same sweet tone:

"O My beloved son that is called a bird"

"O My beloved son that is called a bird"

"O My beloved son that is called a bird"

"O My beloved son..."

The father looked at the young grown man and said:

"O my son I wanted to see the difference, and so I have. When you were small your voice was a pleasure; to see you speak brought joy and laughter to me and your mother. Now as I have become old and weak my voice is

Not so sweet to you, it does not bring that happiness I wished to see..."

Allahu Akbar!

How many parents are the victims of verbal and sometimes physical abuse from their own offspring?

Let them be heard by all, in no uncertain terms, the words of the best of mankind Muhammad bin Abdullah Sallallahu Alayhi Wasallam:

"Allah ta'ala delays whatever he wishes from the punishments of various sins, except the sin of disobeying the parents for verily Allah ta'ala afflicts the punishment in this world before a person dies."

(Tabarani)

Not long ago my mum went to visit a sick friend in hospital. Adjacent to the friend's bed lay a very old woman who, upon seeing my mum, called her to the bedside. My mum greeted her and asked her how she was, but rather than replying she screamed "Please phone my daughter! Tell her to come and see me!" My mum, quiet aghast, said: "Please tell me what's wrong?"

The old woman was so glad that someone was there who bothered to ask that she immediately launched into her life story: "I was a young beautiful girl who got married off at a young age and was blessed with many children, all of whom I nurtured and brought up with love and affection wishing nothing in return. As my children grew up they were deprived of the shadow of their father who passed away at a very young age. I carried on working and striving to give them the best of everything until I got them all married into good families.

Now I have fallen critically ill and my children don't even want to know me. Just before you came my son arrived with a man from the old people's home. The two of them gesticulated, wrote down my details as if I was not here and were off without a word!"

Look at this! This is just one example out of the thousands happening daily. Pay a visit one day to your local old people's home and see how many parents you see sitting all day doing nothing but gazing out of the windows; why? What happened?

Why did they end up there?

No space in the home?

Or no space in the heart?

We've forgotten bro's and sisters that one day we're gonna become parents (inshallah). It's really up to us to make a change: rather than giving them 'dirties', look at them with love and happiness; with a huge smile across your face.

Ibn Abbas radhiyallahu anhu narrates from the beloved messenger Muhammad (sallallahu alayhi wasallam) that no obedient child looks at his parents with affection except that Allah ta'ala grants him with every look the reward of one accepted Hajj. (Bayhaqi)

Imagine sitting in front of your old man or mother- you can gain Hajj upon Hajj. And these are the things that are gonna save your neck on the Day of Reckoning and get you that everlasting bliss; Jannah.

WHEN YOU WERE 12 YEARS OLD, SHE WARNED YOU NOT TO WATCH CERTAIN TV SHOWS
YOU THANKED HER BY WAITING UNTIL SHE LEFT THE HOUSE...

WHEN YOU WERE 13, SHE SUGGESTED A NICE OUTFIT

YOU THANKED HER BY TELLING HER SHE HAD NO TASTE...

**WHEN YOU WERE 14 SHE PAID FOR A MONTH AWAY AT SUMMER CAMP
YOU THANKED HER BY FORGETTING TO WRITE A SINGLE LETTER...**

**WHEN YOU WERE 15, SHE CAME HOME FROM WORK LOOKING FOR A HUG.
YOU THANKED HER BY HAVING YOUR BEDROOM DOOR LOCKED...**

**WHEN YOU WERE 16, SHE WAS EXPECTING AN IMPORTANT PHONE CALL
YOU THANKED BY BEING ON THE PHONE ALL NIGHT,,,**

Alqamah (radhiyallahu anhu). Who was he?

Let me tell you, he was one of the Companions of our Beloved Messenger (sallallahu alayhi wasallam)! He had fallen critically ill and was breathing his last breaths. The surrounding Companions were instructing him to read the kalimah as his last words.

But... but he just could not utter the words.

Huh! You'll say "Why on earth could a companion not read the kalimah?"

Well read on...

The other Companions got worried and rushed to the Saviour of Mankind (sallallahu alayhi wasallam). He, sallallahu alayhi wasallam, immediately diagnosed the problem and asked for his mum. Upon her arrival the Messenger sallallahu alayhi wasallam inquired from her the state of her son. She said "He is a very pious individual praying his salah and observing his fasts… but… there is one thing that he has hurt me greatly by.. He always prefers his wife before me and for this I am upset with Alqamah."

The Messenger sallallahu alayhi wasallam encouraged her to forgive him but she declined, saying the pain was too great.

The Companions were then ordered by the Messenger sallallahu alayhi wasallam to gather firewood. The mother, perplexed asked "What are you doing?"

The Prophet (sallallahu alayhi wasallam) replied "The punishment of this world is much less than the punishment of the Hereafter." Being first and foremost a mother, she changed her mind and cried "No! Please I forgive him; I cannot bear to see my child burn! As these words escaped her lips Alqamah's (radhiyallahu anhu) lips began reciting the kalimah and with these words he passed away…(Reported in Musnad Ahmad and Tabarani)

So, guys and girls out there reading this, it's no joke!

Here we are looking at a Companion who could not recite the kalimah because of the unhappiness of his mother. Think!

It's never too late. If our parents are still alive then let's make the most of it with them and give them all the love, affection and care we have. Coz believe you me you'll find a substitute to everything you lose but you can go to the East or the West and you'll never find a second for your real parents...
If our parents have departed from this world the least we can do is cry for them and make du'a to Allah to elevate their status in Paradise.

Let's try our best: if we go wrong sometime just clear it up by apologising sincerely and starting again. We really have to if we want that bird in Jannah! I mean the one you get to eat not the other one! But I guess you could include that one as well. (Sorry for the lame joke but you have to understand the seriousness of this topic, that's why I made such a joke so you cry even more...)

WHEN YOU WERE 17 YEARS OLD, SHE TAUGHT YOU TO DRIVE HER CAR
YOU THANKED HER BY TAKING IT EVERY CHANCE YOU COULD...

WHEN YOU WERE 18, SHE CRIED AT YOUR HIGH SCHOOL GRADUATION
YOU THANKED HER BY STAYING OUT PARTYING UNTIL DAWN...

WHEN YOU WERE 19, SHE PAID FOR YOUR TUITION FEES DROVE YOU TO
CAMPUS AND CARRIED YOUR BAGS
YOU THANKED HER BY SAYING GOOD-BYE OUTSIDE THE DORM SO YOU
WOULDN'T BE EMBARRASSED IN FRONT OF YOUR FRIENDS...

WHEN YOU WERE 20, SHE ASKED YOU WHERE YOU WERE SPENDING
YOUR MONEY
YOU THANKED HER BY SAYING, "IT'S NONE OF YOUR BUSINESS..."

WHEN YOU WERE 21, SHE SUGGESTED CERTAIN CAREER PATHS FOR YOUR
FUTURE
YOU THANKED HER BY SAYING, "I DON'T WANT TO END UP LIKE YOU..."

WHEN YOU WERE 22, SHE HUGGED YOU AT YOU UNIVERSITY
GRADUATION
YOU THANKED HER BY ASKING WHETHER SHE COULD PAY FOR A TRIP
TO EUROPE...

You know, not long ago parents were taken to be assets, today they are taken as burdens.
"Huh! Not him again!"
"Oh no here she goes again!!"
Yes, what a change, before children would not even raise their heads when talking to their parents, and if they were walking with them they'd walk two steps behind. Today? Forget humility, we look down upon

Them! And forget walking two steps behind: we don't even get time to sit with them... seems weird how teenagers used to be, but they really would do anything to please their parents.

One final story to understand the natural love our mother and father have for us. There was this guy who once fell in love with a girl from school. So deep rooted was the love of this boy that he said "Oh my beloved your order is my command..." She said "How do I know you're going to be loyal to me and never dump me? The boy told her to put him to the test and she would see. His so called beloved made a nasty request saying that if he loved her he would bring his mother's liver on a plate! (Huh crazy girl she must have been) Anyway whether her statement was serious or not we do not know, but 'love is blind' as they say, and this gaff went and stabbed his own mother. He yanked out the liver and brought it back to his girl. On the way he stumbled and fell. From the liver came a voice: "Oh my son are you ok? You're not hurt are you?"

Allahu Akbar!

The girl was shocked and said you murderer I don't wanna know you! get lost!"

So readers and friends, I know it's been a long chapter I'll just end with a few key points on how to make the best relations with our parents, now that we've realised (inshallah) that we have to serve them.

Try your best to keep them happy 24/7. If they trouble and shout at you which doesn't often happen (unless you've just broken your mum's china plate or smashed your dad's car window with the footie!) then still the command is to be nice towards them.

Make du'a for them. Here is a du'a from the Qur'an which Allah has taught us to make for our parents. Try to learn it and pray it regularly:

'RABBIR HAMHUMA KAMA RABBAYANEE

SAGHEERA'

(Surah 17 Ayah 24)

"Oh Allah have mercy on them as they cherished me in my childhood."

Try your absolute best to fulfil all their desires and wishes, and if they do tell you to do something that you just can't do then don't say "Get lost!" or "In your dreams!" rather better humble yourself. Allah ta'ala commanded us centuries ago to lower ourselves in front of our parents and to not even tut. So let's try to be sweet, we should be saying something like "My dear mum I'd really love to do it but you know I just can't at the moment because... and I truly do hope you will excuse and forgive me this time."

Its up to us, a bit of sugar on the tongue and some will power will get us their happiness and in turn the pleasure of the Almighty Allah.

Next time your old man tells you something, think twice....!

WHEN YOU WERE 23, SHE GAVE YOU FURNITURE FOR YOUR FIRST APARTMENT.
YOU THANKED HER BY TELLING YOUR FRIENDS HOW UGLY IT WAS...

WHEN YOU WERE 24, SHE FOUND A PROSPECTIVE SPOUSE FOR YOU AND ASKED ABOUT YOUR PLANS FOR THE FUTURE
YOU THANKED HER BY GLARING AND GROWLING, "MUUHHTHER, PLEASE!"

WHEN YOU WERE 25, SHE HELPED PAY FOR YOUR WEDDING, AND SHE CRIED AND TOLD YOU HOW DEEPLY SHE LOVED YOU

YOU THANKED HER BY MOVING HALFWAY ACROSS THE COUNTRY...

**WHEN YOU WERE 30, SHE CALLED WITH SOME ADVICE ON THE BABY
YOU THANKED HER BY TELLING HER, "THINGS ARE DIFFERENT NOW..."**

**WHEN YOU WERE 40, SHE CALLED TO REMIND YOU OF A RELATIVE'S
CRITICAL ILLNESS. YOU THANKED HER BY SAYING YOU WERE "REALLY
BUSY RIGHT NOW.."**

**WHEN YOU WERE 50; SHE FELL ILL AND NEEDED YOU TO TAKE CARE OF
HER
YOU THANKED HER BY READING ABOUT THE BURDEN PARENTS BECOME
TO THEIR CHILDREN...**

**AND THEN ONE DAY SHE QUIETLY DIED... AND
EVERYTHING YOU NEVER DID CAME CRASHING DOWN
LIKE THUNDER...**

There's no substitute for parents. Cherish every single moment. Though at times they may not be the best of friends, may not agree with our thoughts, they are your parents! They will be there for you... to listen to your woes, your bragging, your frustrations, etc. Ask yourself... have you put aside enough time for them, to listen to her "blues" of working in the kitchen, his tiredness and fatigue. Once gone, only fond memories of the past and regrets will be left...

Jazz?

Rave?

Pop?

Heavy metal?

Rock?

Or just simply Classical...?

So many to choose from, such a wide collection on the market!
Which one do you go for...?
Accept it or not, bro's and sisters the market for music has boomed over the last fifty years. Wherever you go; however you go, you just can't avoid it: it's there playing or blasting away...
Big deal?
I mean what can some sound do to a human?
'Man! I get this buzz when I'm bouncing on the streets with ma earphones plugged in! I look cool! This ain't gonna harm me!' Well the answer is that this so

called sound, has such a profound effect not only on your physical self but on your spiritual being too, so much so that it can be the means of the eradication of the most precious gift: Iman!

Yes that's right our Beloved Messenger(sallallahu alayhi wasallam) has said :

"Music cultivates hypocrisy in the heart just as water grows crops." (Abu Dawud)

Hypocrisy, what is it? Sounds like some rare plant from the Amazon Jungle. Well you could say that, because it is like a plant but a very venomous one whose abode is in the lowest stage of Jahannum.

The Qur'an very explicitly has stated:

The Hypocrites will be in the lowest depths of Jahannum; no helper will you find for them.
(Surah 4 Verse 145)

(Hypocrisy (Nifaq) is to be a Muslim outwardly but a disbeliever inside.)

Jahannum! Think it's a joke? More detail will be discussed in later parts but just a rough idea...:

Abu Huriarah(radhiyallahu anhu) narrates from the Messenger (peace be upon Him) that Jahannam was burnt for a thousand years until it became red, then it was burnt for another thousand years till it became white and for a further thousand years it was burnt till it became black, and now it is black like the darkness of the night. (Tirmidhi)

Abu Saeed Khudree (radhiyallahu anhu) has narrated that the Messenger(peace be upon Him) said that if a hammer from Jahannum were to be placed on the earth and the entire human race along with the jinns were asked to carry it; they would not be able to lift it. (Ahmad)

Abdullah bin Harith (radhiyallahu anhu) narrates from the Messenger (peace be upon Him) that in Jahannum the snakes shall be extremely long: when they bite their poison shall be felt for seventy years; the scorpions shall be the size of mules and their sting shall be felt for 40 years. (Ahmad)

Think you can face that?   Not me! See ya later
alligator…

The Qur'an, this fault-free book of guidance: what has
it called this 'music' ?
   "Lead to destruction (Here, Allah is talking to the
   big Shaytan, Iblees) those who you can among them
             through your voice…" (Verse 64 surah17)

It has called music the voice of Shaytan: the voice of
the devil! Sounds eerie huh? Not so innocent any more?
Now I want you to make the decision: is it really worth
it? I mean what pleasure can one get from listening to
those beats and drums while your Creator your
Sustainer is angry? Remember He has the power to
make you lose your hearing should he wish!
Then? Who's gonna help us?

It's just a bit like drugs ain't it? Go on a high for a while
then 'wham!' back to normality and reality. You do
remember all that stuff from Part One don't you?

And here and now I call for your attention once again. Allow me to introduce you to: The Physical Harms of MUSIC...

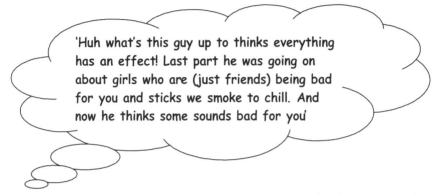

'Huh what's this guy up to thinks everything has an effect! Last part he was going on about girls who are (just friends) being bad for you and sticks we smoke to chill. And now he thinks some sounds bad for you'

Well if you're thinking the above then look mate- I'm not sitting here and making all this stuff up you know. I've got better things to do. My teacher has written a wonderful book called 'Music Exposed' so with his permission I quote to you some of the physical harms of music.

Music: Art of combining sounds into coherent perceptual experience, typically in accordance with fixed patterns and for an aesthetic purpose.

(The Hutchinson Encyclopaedia, New unabridged Edition) Got that? Don't worry, me neither...

The word 'music' is derived from the Greek 'Mousike,' which at the time covered all the arts occupied by the Muses (Greek Goddesses in Greek Mythology).

It's really amazing that Our Creator only forbids that which is bad and harmful to us and allows only that which is good and beneficial. Physiological experiments confirm that music not only affects the brain, but affects every organ of one's body. There is a close relationship between music and bodily movements. Come on you must've seen (or maybe experienced yourself) the tapping of feet, fingers when the beats begin? Yes? No?

"The loud sounds and bright lights of today are tremendous indoctrination (teaching) tools. It is possible to modify the human chemical structure with the right concentration of frequencies. What kind of beat makes you tap your foot? What beat makes you curl your fist and strike? (Gary Allen: The Music)

'...different types of music are used to influence shoppers in various ways- easy listening music to relax customers, upbeat tunes to speed up shoppers during busy periods and, in the run up to Christmas, carols to lull people into the festive mood.' (Leicester Mail 22nd Oct 1998)

"We are moving into their minds and so are most of the newer groups." (Mick Jagger of Rolling Stones)

"...the influence of music as a catalyst or trigger for anti-social behaviour, sexual arousal, is all too apparent.' 'The visual element is personified in the mass exploitation of Women through photography. We have a controlling creature beyond any unit, we have Madonna, and we have Spice girls...' (A.W. Woolsey: Music for Markets)

The following is based on a television program produced for Channel Four by Equinox, entitled: 'Rave: the New World.'

'It hits you and it bombards you and it breaks down any of those barriers...'

'It just pounds your ears with a 4/4 rhythm of up to 180 beats a minute...' 'At the heart is Ecstasy, but the pleasure of rave has its price. It kills!'

There's so much to say about this one word; 'music' but I don't wanna bore you.. if you've already made your mind up to stop listening to music.   But please, think! Allah has revealed His Beautiful book The Qur'an: is that not more worthy for a Muslim to listen to than these silly people's voice? In your MP3's and now there's Mp4's (who knows by the time you read this there might be MP5's and 6's) can't we download the recitation of the Qur'an rather than the tracks many teens have nowadays?

Just a little more before we kill this chapter off totally.

Computer Hypnosis: Sounds and Pictures.

Everyone knows all those colours and pictures that are

screened alongside music or audio tracks, well they a'int no innocent. Check this out! The guys that do this stuff are called 'Techno Artists', and one Matt Black, a techno Artist, says:

'Really we want to turn people on and get inside their heads. With the interactive element we want to lure people into our world...'

Hey I'm not letting any Matt Black into my head! Don't know about you guys...

Weird stuff huh!

The actual process used by the Music World as a way of controlling and influencing the minds of the general public is 'Backtracking or Back masking.'

One way back masking

The lyrics of the song are sung backwards. When these nonsensical phrases are reversed, a meaningful message is deciphered.

Example: The Single by Black Oak of Arkansas.

'When Electricity comes to Arkansas.'

Forward Lyrics (the one that is heard): Natas, Natas, Natas Sidrol

Backward: (Got it) Satan, Satan is Lord.

Backtracking

This one is a little hard to grasp but what happens is that they record a normal lyric backward that can only be picked up by your sub conscious mind. If you want to hear the actual message then you gotta reverse the whole thing.

Examples: Michael Jackson Track: Beat it.

Album: Thriller

Forward: They'll kick you, they'll beat you, then they'll tell you, it's fair, so beat it, but you wanna be bad, just beat it.

(Once you've backtracked this.)

Backward: Believe in Satan, people all worship Satan, I do believe it was Satan in me.

Huh! Imagine that, and it's not fake this stuff. I remember in one of my study classes we got a track on the computer and backtracked it. The whole class heard the dark messages with their own ears!

Eagles: 'Hotel California'

Forward: And I was thinking to myself, this could be heaven, this could be Hell. Then she lit up a candle and she showed me the way. There would be voices down the corridor; I thought I heard them say...

Backwards: I do not believe in Jesus... Here Satan had organised his own religion when he knows he shouldn't have, it was delicious, he puts it in a vat, he fixed it for his son, which he gives away.

Look at the choice of the song title, it is a well known fact that the Hotel California is the first satanic church, on California Street, California. Many pop artists have confessed their connection to this church...

Madonna, Title: Like A Prayer

Forward: When you call my name its like a little prayer

I'm down on my knees, I wanna take you there in the midnight hour...
Backward: O hear us Satan...

Eerie stuff this is. Can't wait to finish this chapter. Can feel my fingers tapping away... (On the keyboard I mean).

Let's have a few more real life incidents.

In a book called 'Don't mess with my Music' over a hundred examples are quoted where individuals have acted on the music they were listening to. A 15 Year old boy, who killed his mother, was questioned in an interview.

Interviewer: If you could say anything to young people that might keep them from going the same road you have gone, what advice would you offer?

Boy: There is one thing I would say and that is: 'Don't go

anywhere near that Heavy Metal Music'... I listened to heavy metal from a young age because I really enjoyed the beat and loud aggressive style, but my problems all started when I started listening to the lyrics. They were singing about worshipping Satan, about getting supernatural powers and about mocking Jesus. When I heard all these things I wanted to know more. So I started to get hold of books on the occult (satanic worship) and witchcraft. Then I got involved with a group in school that was into satanic practices. We got into some pretty heavy things. But it was the Music more than anything else that gripped me. I used to go up to my bedroom and listen hours on end. My walls were covered with heavy metal music posters. My folks (parents) never knew what I was listening to and I don't know if they even cared. I even heard a song about killing your mother, I can't remember a lot of what happened when I killed my mother, but I can remember talking in a strange deep voice. Even though it's been 10 long months since I've listened to any heavy metal music, I still have a lot of words of these songs going through my mind all day long. Sometimes I wake up at three in the morning with the Iron Maiden song:'Number of Beast' going through my brain...'

What a sad story. Please, my dear brothers and sisters let us learn from others. How many teens are out there at this very moment lost in their own world with no one to turn to, no one to help, messed up inside and outside? Let us change now before it's too late to regret. May Allah ta'ala help us all.

The group Judas Priest was taken to court by two American families who claimed that the song 'Better by You, Better by me' drove their two healthy young sons to suicide. This song was found to contain subliminal chants of 'Do it, Do it'. Psychologists admitted that: 'if you listen to this record at full volume, you will feel compelled to kill yourself.' (Evening Standard, March 1995)

Rock star David Crosbie confided in an interview regarding music and backtracking: 'I figured the only thing to do was to swipe (brainwash) the kids, I'm talking about changing the value systems, removing them from their parents and the world.'

'Madonna, Spice Girls and Britney Spears have exploited the market with obsessive sexual lyrics and similar stage acts not short of pornography.' Behind the glitzy and glam image of pop music is a dark and sinister tale of Satanism, Paranoia, unhappiness and loneliness...' (Siraj Ibn Yusuf Lambat: Music Exposed)

That's it folks. If you decide to stop then remember you have made your Creator, your Sustainer your Nourisher happy and his (and your) enemy Shaytan sad. I know it's hard, but ask Allah to help you.

Chapter

Three

GROWING

In life there are two main stages: childhood and adulthood. These are also known as the time before maturity (na baligh) and the time after maturity (baligh). In this chapter we shall be discussing the bridge that takes one from being a child to being an adult.

So how does one actually know and realise they are crossing this bridge?

Hmm... listen attentively; sorry read attentively (so lame I can't walk. Get it?) before we begin to explain and discuss this very delicate issue, one thing needs to be made clear.

Shyness in aspects of religion cannot be tolerated. So don't feel reluctant or shy to ask about these things, coz you know what? It happens to everyone. Many parents, due to their own upbringing shy away from such topics and fail to educate their offspring of what changes occur in their bodies as they grow. This is not the fault of the parents but, like I've said before, the environment has a great effect on a person's actions. So that's why I'm telling you so inshallah when you become parents, (ameen) grandparents (ameen) great grandparents (ameen) (shall I carry on? One more.) And great great grandparents (ameen) then you can explain to your progeny all this kinda stuff.

For a boy, the time of maturity is when he has a wet dream, and is from the age of 12 upwards.

For a girl ,it is when her periods start, which can happen anytime after the age of 9.

There is no maximium age to all this, if these things don't happen by the age of 15 then Islamically you are counted as a mature person.

(The issue of periods and other girl related topics shall be discussed in a separate book which is to be published soon inshallah by An- Nasihah Publications entitled; THE HIJAB, by Sister Rehmat. So keep an eye out)

What is a wet dream? Well basically, to cut the details a person goes to sleep and sees himself with the opposite gender and upon awakening finds that his clothes are wet around his private parts. Sometimes he/she might not see anything and still find this in the morning. Both examples are classified as wet dreams, scientifically known as 'nocturnal emissions of semen'. We'll mention semen on the next page.

Got that so far? Good! Ok so someone had a wet dream now what does he have to do?

The answer is that Gusl is obligatory upon him before he prays any salah or Qur'an: he has to wash himself.

There are three main things in gusl. Make sure you know 'em:

1) Rinse the mouth thoroughly, (gargle).

2) Clean the nose throroughly.

3) Wash each part of the body in such a way that no hair is left dry. After which you are pure and clean.

Hey does that mean when we get this dream, whatever it's called, we're in a state of impurity?

Yep, that's right. The liquid that comes out is impure

and makes bathing compulsory. There are three main liquids that come out of the private parts other than urine. I've put them all in a nice chart for you guys.

Name of Liquids

Mani (Semen)

When: Due to a wet dream or when having relationship with spouse.

What to do: Gusl (bath)

Description: Thick liquid, comes out in excess usually silvery white for men and pale yellowish for women.

Mazi(PreseminalFluid)

In non scientific terms this is known as love juice.

When: Due to excitement coz of kissing etc... (Can't give too much detail. Hope you understand.)

What to do: Washing of the part, and wudu Only.

Description: Sticky. Only a few drops come out. Colourless.

Wadi

(Don't know the name in English, sorry mate.)

When: When force is exerted on the body, whilst passing stool or carrying a heavy load.

What to do: Washing of the part, and wudu Only. Description: Looks very similar to semen except that very few drops come out.

Ok hope you got all that. Like I said in the beginning this is a very delicate chapter and somethings just need to be explained; now there remains one final thing, well I wouldn't call it a 'thing' but anyway let's not get into all that.   So this thing is a problem many teenagers face on their journey of life after passing the bridge of Maturity (O yeah I forgot to congratulate you guys for becoming men and women! You're not kids anymore, please try to remember that...) This problem, ladies and gentlemen is such a big problem but only a few take it seriously...
Right let me just tell you instead of going round in circles (Phew...)

What happens when you become mature is that, like you already know, your natural inclination (I said natural, so chill, you're not abnormal or bad if you feel this way: it happens to everyone) increases to the max. Your bodily desires attract you to the opposite gender and sometimes sudden arousals take place inside the body to touch each other. (This particular issue of girls and boys intermingling has been discussed in Part One.) When this is not possible (because of the age or because you can't marry that young) then, dear brothers and sisters, what Shaytan tells a young teen is basically 'do it yourself!' It might sound eeh! Do it yourself? What is this, some D.I.Y job? Listen very carefully because this can be a factor which can be stopping you from having children in the future.

With all the nudity and immorality that is spread across the net, the mags, the newspapers and the big box; (The TV), a young girl or boy can begin to view all this with lust and desire. In the process he or she can begin to rub their private parts with their own hands. This action is called masturbation! Mr or Mrs Foolish thinks that this is a way of fulfilling their desires! Never. Be warned! This action has effects worse than anything I have mentioned (hey worse than smoking? Yep!) Furthermore he or she slowly becomes addicted to this filthy act. In boys it involves forcing out Mani (semen) through unnatural means, resulting in him becoming the victim of a condition called premature ejaculation. This means that, during love-making with his wife, his semen comes out too quickly. This can make it difficult for conception (Producing babies).

Teen: Woah! Chill! That was a bit too heavy!

Teach: I know but you had to understand it very clearly.

Teen: Ok what else happens if you do this masturbation stuff?

Teach: Well the following are a few of the many side effects: It weakens the heart, brain, liver and stomach. It affects the growth of the limbs especially the outer part of the urethra. It causes an excessive loss of blood. Remember it takes approx 40-80 drops of blood to produce one drop of sprem.

Teen: As if?

Teach: Believe you me these are not just made up they have been proven.

Teen: Ok and?

Teach: Your wife will like you less coz she won't be satisfied by you. There are many other physical illnesses such as always feeling tired. An increase in nervous agitation, loss of confidence. Above all though, you earn the wrath and anger of Allah. Severe punishment has been mentioned in the Ahadith regarding such people. Semen, sperm, mani- whatever you call it- is that liquid through which Allah creates the Human being. And you are spilling that. Doesn't that make such a person a murderer??

Teen: hey teach that's kinda true?

Teach: dah!

Teen: What if some gaff has been doing it for many years then?

Teach: Then tell him to stop right away. Just like when you stop smoking your lungs begin to clear up. Similarly once you stop this filthy act, your body, through the will of Allah, goes through a natural heeling process. It could take years and in some cases medication might be needed. Homeopathic medication is known to be good for such illnesses. Remember your friends might say chill man just do it! But remember say no! It's addictive and it's a killer!

Teen: Ok I get the message ill just txt him.

"Hey goose stp doin dat stuf v do coz it ain't gud 4 u. u wnt be able 2 get a hapy wfe!

Reply:Lol.. shut it ay... Its my life!

Teen: No it aint Allah gve u dat body n it ain't made for dat!

Reply:Ooh sum1s changing...

Teen: Yeah coz I understan why I ve bin made ."

Wat u made 4?

Teen:2 make my Allah hapy!

Teach: Mashallah.

Think if you become mature at 9 or 12 then its really approx. 10 years of patience till you get married, then u can have so much fun and be happy too coz you'll know al the back of your head that you had a pure life, a pure teen life...

Chapter
Four

FASHION

Fashion, a word that has no stability, can fluctuate can change more quickly than the British weather! One minute the 70's style was laughed upon and then suddenly it came back; everyone's wearing bellbottoms and flared trousers. We're back into the past. Then boom! A new fashion emerges, a new style comes out and every1 wants to wear it, do it and have it. Look at the crazy wave of earrings and studs. Ok, we know the ears but suddenly every part of the body supposedly looks attractive with a piece of jewellery embedded on. The tongue, the lips & the belly button. The latest one I heard of was in the eyes! Through an operation some fanatics of fashion have a stud implanted in their eye! She wont have to make him meet her eyes he'll be gawping at her thinking "what a silly goose!"

In the Oxford Dictionary, fashion has been defined as: 'Style in clothes, hairstyle etc..., popular at a particular time.'

In this very unstable chapter we shall be discussing some of the practices rampant in my time, so if you're reading this in later years you'll have to reflect on the evidence of fashion in your own time, because one thing is for sure it won't stay the same...

Let's start with the most respected and honoured part of the human body: the face. How has this fashion stepped on our faces?

Eyebrows- especially for girls (that's at this time maybe boys might fancy it soon who knows...) the shaving or shaping of eyebrows and sometimes drawing artificial eyebrows with a pencil... Ever seen it boys? If not then mashallah you've been practising on the first chapter by keeping your gazes low. If yes then umm... no comments.

The Qur'an says:

'Let there be no change in the work of Allah.'

(Surah 30 Ayah 30)

Abdullah Ibn Masud (May Allah be pleased with him) has said that Allah has cursed those women who pluck their eyebrows. (Bukhari and Muslim)(Plucking includes shaping and removing.)

The curse of Allah ta'ala: now what does cursing mean? Well I checked the literal meaning and it goes like this: "The distancing of a servant from the mercy of Allah with His anger.'

Imagine Allah pushes us away in a state that He is angry with us! Allah ta'ala has created us in the best of forms. May Allah allow us to understand. Amen.

Beautifying is totally different that is not changing the creation of Allah, so girls don't start throwing your vanity cases away. You can wear all those necklaces and earrings. I'm talking to the girls by the way, boys, for you earrings and necklaces and chains are strictly forbidden! Yes, strictly, because you know why? Because you're a boy, a man, and this stuffs for girls and women. Sadly, in the 21st century people have forgotten the gender differences, walking on a street you see this boy coming towards you, you begin to think "hey do I know him?" From where? As he comes closer oops it's a girl! Ever happened?

Allahu Akbar how much have we changed? When the

girls were supposed to be covered from head to toe today we see them becoming more and more uncovered. And the lads? Well they wanna become street sweepers nowadays coz their trouser legs are just getting longer and longer.

The Messenger, (peace be upon him) has cursed the men who imitate women and the women who imitate men (Bukhari)

Now, since the idea of covering has come up, let us discuss the aspect of purdah and niqab.

A request to the boys not to skip this part, for one day, inshallah, when you become husbands and fathers then you can explain this to your spouses and daughters...

OK, why cover up? The most commonly asked question? Have you ever seen a decent-minded human being walking the street flashing a £50 note? (I said decent-minded, remember).

No? but why not? Its such a nice crisp, flat note wouldn't it be nice if people could see it and touch it?

In the case of Islam you girls are a million times more precious then a flimsy paper note! When a single note is wrapped, zipped and put into your safest pocket then why should we let or daughters, our sisters and our mothers become the objects of lust and desire for evil eyes? Just like a pearl is protected in its oyster similarly a Muslimah covers her beauty to protect her body! That's it, no other wisdom.

Tell me is this oppression? Or is oppression that a girl is displayed and a once upon a time modest girl loses her chastity to become the tool of money making schemes, appearing on bill boards, TV ads, magazines and wherever else they need 'em? This young girl is stripped of her modesty, her self esteem and her self respect. Do you want to be that cheap? Think, dear sisters, if this model were to have an accident (Allah forbid) and come up with a scar across her face, would she still have her job? Would guys still drool at her? You see, it's all on face value Islam gives you more than this. Like a banana is protected by its thick skin,

When it is opened and left, look at the quality. How does it deteriorate? Becoming the prey of paedophiles and men who care nothing about the dignity of women, only caring for their whims and desires. In such a ruthless society for a Muslimah to veil herself is surely a great achievement. Despite all her non Muslim friends going around showing their bodies. I Maryam, I Ayesha, I Sumayyah, I Zahra will stand up and shall not let my body be sold for a few comments: "Wow!" "You look awesome!" " How sleek and smooth is your hair!" This Maryam, this Sumayyah and this Ayesha has so much honour and respect in the sight of Allah, coz even though she posseses the means to enjoy the artificial praises she covers up her whole body only for Allah!

Her real status will only be recognised on the Day of Judgement.

So, my dear sisters, pluck up the courage from this moment and go to the nearest shop and lay your hands on that ticket to Jannah; your first nikab (face covering), hijab (head scarf) and abaya (long dress). Don't worry what people will say, a day shall most definitely come in your life when you will thank Allah for granting you the ability. A day when you feel your life and body to be clean and pure, and when you begin to feel 'expensive,' and not 'cheap'.

Check this article out:

Why I Shed Bikini for Niqab
The New Symbol of Women's Liberation
By
Sara Bokker*

"I am an American woman who was born in the midst of America's Heartland. I grew up, just like any other girl, being fixated with the glamour of life in the big city. Eventually, I moved to Florida and on to South Beach of Miami, a hotspot for those seeking the glamorous life. Naturally, I did what most average Western girls do. I focused on my appearance and appeal, basing my self-worth on how much attention I got from others. I worked out religiously and became a personal trainer, acquired an upscale waterfront residence, became a regular exhibiting beach-goer and was able to attain a living-in-style kind of life.

Years went by, only to realize that my scale of self-fulfilment and happiness slid down the more I progressed in my feminine appeal. I was a slave to fashion. I was a hostage to my looks. As the gap continued to progressively widen between my self-fulfilment and lifestyle, I sought refuge from alcohol and parties to meditation, activism, and alternative religions, only to have the little gap widen to what seemed like a valley. I eventually realized it all was merely a pain killer rather than an effective remedy.

By now it was September 11, 2001. As I witnessed the ensuing barrage on Islam, Islamic values and culture, and the infamous declaration of the new crusade, I started to notice something called Islam. Up until that point, all I had associated with Islam was women covered in tents, wife beaters, harems, and a world of terrorism. As a feminist libertarian, and an activist who was pursuing a better world for all, my path crossed with that of another activist who was already at the lead of indiscriminately furthering causes of reform and justice for all. I joined in the ongoing campaigns of my new mentor which included, at the time, election reform and civil rights, among others. Now my new activism was fundamentally different. Instead of selectively advocating justice only to some, I learned that ideals such as justice, freedom, and respect are essentially universal and that one's own good and the common good are not in conflict. For the first time, I knew what "all people are created equal" really means. But most importantly, I learned that it only takes faith to see the world as one and to see the unity in creation. One day I came across a book that is negatively stereotyped in the West--The Holy Qur'an. I was first attracted by the style and approach of the Qur'an, and then intrigued by its outlook on existence, life, creation, and the relationship between Creator and creation. I found the Qur'an to be a very insightful address to heart and soul without the need for an interpreter or pastor.

Eventually I hit a moment of truth: my new-found self-fulfilling activism was nothing more than merely embracing a faith called Islam where I could live in peace as a functional Muslim.

I bought a beautiful long gown and head cover resembling the Muslim woman's dress code and I walked down the same streets and neighbourhoods where only days earlier I had walked in my shorts, bikini, or elegant western business attire. Although the people, the faces, and the shops were all the same, one thing was remarkably distinct-the peace at being a woman I experienced for the very first time. I felt as if the chains had been broken and I was finally free. I was delighted with the new looks of wonder on people's faces in place of the looks of a hunter watching his prey I had once sought. Suddenly a weight had been lifted off my shoulders. I no longer spent all my time consumed with shopping, makeup, getting my hair done, and working out. Finally, I was free.

Of all places, I found my Islam at the heart of what some call the most scandalous place on earth, which makes it all the more dear and special.

While content with hijab I became curious about niqab, seeing an increasing number of Muslim women in it. At the time, my hijab consisted of a head scarf that covered all my hair except for my face, and a loose long black gown called abaya that covered all my body from neck to toe.

A year-and-a-half passed, and I told my Muslim husband, whom I married after I reverted to Islam, I wanted to wear niqab. My reason, was that I felt it would be more pleasing to Allah, the Creator, increasing my feeling of peace at being more modest. He supported my decision and took me to buy an isdaal, a loose black gown that covers from head to toe, and niqab, which covers all my head and face except for my eyes.

Soon enough, news started breaking about politicians, Vatican clergymen, libertarians, and so-called human rights and freedom activists condemning hijab at times, and niqab at others as being oppressive to women, an obstacle to social integration, and more recently, as an Egyptian official called it--a sign of backwardness.

I find it to be a blatant hypocrisy when western governments and so-called human rights groups rush to defend woman's rights when some governments impose a certain dress code on women, yet such freedom fighters look the other way when women are being deprived of their rights, work, and education just because they choose to exercise their right to wear niqab or hijab.

Today I am still a feminist, but a Muslim feminist, who calls on Muslim women to assume their responsibilities in providing all the support they can for their husbands to be good Muslims. To raise their children as upright Muslims so they may be beacons of light for all humanity once again. To enjoin good--any good--and to forbid evil--any evil. To speak righteousness and to speak up against all ills. To fight for our right to wear niqab or hijab and to please our Creator whichever way we chose. But just as importantly to carry our experience with niqab or hijab to fellow women who may never have had the chance to understand what wearing niqab or hijab means to us and why we so dearly embrace it.

Most of the women I know wearing niqab are Western reverts, some of whom are not even married. Others wear niqab without full support of either family or surroundings. What we all have in common is that it is the personal choice of each and every one of us, which none of us is willing to surrender. Willingly or unwillingly, women are bombarded with styles of dressing-in- little-to- nothing virtually in every means of communication everywhere in the world.

Yesterday, the bikini was the symbol of my liberty, when in actuality it only liberated me from my spirituality and true value as a respectable human being.

I couldn't be happier to shed my bikini in South Beach and the glamorous Western lifestyle to live in peace with my Creator and enjoy living among fellow humans as a worthy person. It is why I choose to wear niqab, and why I will die defending my inalienable right to wear it. 'You don't know what you are missing.'

Sara Bokker is a former actress/model/fitness instructor and activist. Currently, Sara is Director of Communications at the March for Justice, a co-founder of The Global Sisters Network, and producer of the infamous Shock & Awe Gallery.

Right boys your turn! No jokes! it's time to pull our socks up... read very carefully and don't let Shaytan fool you! The beard!

Yes today we think it's cool to look like girls, hairless faces!It's a sign of femininity man! I met this Muslim postal worker with a beard he said that his colleague once asked him "doesn't your wife mind man, with all the hair on your face? Subhanallah you know what he said? He said "My wife found me too feminine; she thought I was a lady when I used to shave. Now with a beard I look and feel like a man!"

And you know if you look into History nearly all men used to keep beards. The Nation of Lut (alayhis salam) were the first civilisation to initiate this shaving of beards and do you know who they were? Majority were homosexuals! May Allah protect us!

Remember lads, think: is it worth it? Again ask yourself who am I living for? People? Or for myself and Allah?

It was the sixth year of Hijra and the Messenger (Peace be upon him) decided to invite the rulers of the world to Islam. Letters were sent to Hercules of Rome, Kisra Perwez, Emperor of Persia, the King of Abyssinia and, finally, to Maqawqis, the King of Egypt.

All these leaders respected and honoured the message except for the Persian king, Kisra. He tore the letter to pieces and sent a message to his governor in Yemen, Bazan. He ordered him to arrest the Beloved Prophet (peace be upon him) (nauzubillah) and to bring him to him. Bazan sent two of his greatest warriors to Madinah Munawwarah. When they arrived they asked "Where does your king live? We see no palace or mansion?" The companions explained that their leader Muhammad (Peace be upon him) was a simple man and lived in an ordinary house like them. So, these two warriors came before the beloved Messenger (Peace be upon him). Now their state was this: that apart from long moustaches they were totally clean shaven! The beloved Messenger (Peace be upon him) could not bear to look at their appearances so he turned his face away and asked them who told them to do that? (meaning shave their beards) They replied our lord (kisra) had done so, so the Messenger (Peace be upon him) quickly replied that his Rabb (Allah) had told him to lengthen the beard and shorten the moustache.

The story carries on that the beloved Messenger (Peace be upon him) told them that Kisra had been killed. With this in mind, they set out on their journey in a state of shock, upon reaching Yemen the news came that indeed kisra had been murdered at that very time the messenger peace be upon him told them!

(Reported in Tabarani, Hayatus Sahabah and Al Bidaya)

Let us stop for a moment to think! Who were these two warriors? They were not Muslims. Yet despite this, the Messenger (Peace be upon him) could not bear to look at

Their faces. Dear brothers, for Allah's sake, ponder for a moment if on the Day of Judgement we present ourselves to our messenger and what if he turns his face away from us? Then where shall we go? To which girl shall we go for help on that day? The day regarding which the Qur'an has said:

"That day shall a man flee from his own brother, and from his mother and his father and from his wife and children. Each one of them that day will have enough concern (of his own) to make him indifferent to the others" (surah 80 verses 34-37)

There are some who watch things happen, some wait for things to happen while others make things happen! Let us be of this third group and bring a change into our lives. You're intelligent, go for it: reason and balance the advantages and disadvantages of following the Sunnah. I leave it to you...

Chapter
Five

FRIENDS

I'm not talking about the American sit-com 'Friends' in case you're wondering. The word 'human' in Arabic is 'insanun', derived from the root word 'anisa' which means to find solace, peace and comfort from others. Hence it is the nature of all human beings to find happiness when in the company of others, i.e. friends.

If we all were to have our own cocoon with no humans around us then it would be impossible to breathe, sorry to live!

When Adam (alayhis salam) was created and put in Jannah he felt lonely. So Allah ta'ala made for him Hawa (alayhas salam) who became his wife (I said this coz u might think its ok to have a girlfriend.) Remember your best friend should be (and inshallah will be) your wife. But what we are talking about is the time before you get to that wonderful moment (happy waiting...)

Are we really to pick our friends like flowers? Does it matter that much who we hang around with?

The beloved of all; Muhammad (sallallahu alayhi wasallam) has said: The example of a good friend is

like a perfume seller, even if he does not give you any
scent you shall most definitely benefit from the
smell and the example of a bad friend is like a
blacksmith, even if your clothes do not get burnt, the
smoke shall definitely touch you. (Reported by
Abdullah ibn Masud in Bukhari, Muslim, Tirmidhi, Ibn
Majah & Nasai)

Subhanallah what a beautiful explanation! Now how on
earth do you know how the mates you hang around with
are good?

Ok! Quite simple. Does he or she have the qualities of a
true Muslim?

Generous?

Forbearing?

Forgiving?

Humble?

Polite?

Always willing to assist others?

Punctual on Salah?

Acts upon the Sunnah?

Tells you when you've done something wrong?

If all the answers to these are 'yes' then Alhamdulillah, you've struck it lucky. You're looking at an ideal friend. If 'no' then you ought to reverse out of the friendship ASAP.

For the beloved Messenger (peace be upon him) has said:
' A Person shall be with whom he loves.' (Bukhari)
Meaning that on the Day of Judgement you shall be raised with the company you kept.

You'll see this in life: a good kid from a good background suddenly meets up with a guy that's into smoking and usually within a couple of months this good guy now becomes a smoker.
WAllahi, dear brothers and sisters it just can't be explained, but whoever you stay with will most definitely affect you.
Maulana Rum (May Allah be pleased with him) has written a beautiful story regarding the effects of bad company. He writes:

Once there was a frog and a mouse who became friends. Their friendship grew as the days and weeks passed until they could not bear the separation and would long to meet and talk to each other at the hours of night when the frog would be deep below the water and the mouse in a quiet place on land. The mouse at once came up with an idea: "Hey why don't we tie a rope to our feet and when you miss me at night you can pull that rope. In that way I'll come straight down to the river and we can never feel that pain of separation?" So this is what they did. It so happened that one day the mouse was walking and a bird flew by. Seeing the mouse scurrying here and there, the bird launched an attack and scooped it up in its long talons. It began to fly away with the mouse, but as it was also tied, the young frog felt itself being yanked up into the sky. The frog looked up and saw its fate. The mouse said: "Sorry mate, you wanted to be my friend!"

The Qur'an explains to us the words of regret a man shall utter on the Day of Judgement:

"And remember that day when the wrongdoer will bite his hands; he will say: 'Oh! Would that I had taken a path with the Messenger." Ah! Woe to me! I wish I had not made so-and-so an intimate friend!"

(Surah 25 Ayah 27-28)

So let us befriend the pious and sit in the company of the ulema (scholars) for as the rain falls and hits the ground all around, similarly when the mercy of Allah descends on these servants we shall most certainly get some portion...

The big box, standing in the corner of millions of homes around the globe. Open Surah Luqman Verse 6. Allah the Almighty states:

"And amongst men are those who purchase tales which cause neglect, to mislead men from the path of Allah without knowledge."

Tales which cause neglect? A recent survey showed that an average teen spends 1100 hours a year viewing this box! If that's not neglect then what else can it be? A most influential teacher lurks in our homes today, teaching us values and lessons we've never dreamt of, in turn causing people to act in weird ways.

Did you hear of the two boys who went and messed their neighbours home on account of watching the game show 'Finders Keepers'? What about the Muslim boy who killed himself coz e wanted to become the Lion King? His parents found this note in his room:

"I have killed myself because I want to become Lion King. Good bye mum and dad, brothers and sisters, Good bye forever."

'Misleading people without knowledge'

The Messenger (peace be upon him) has stated:
'Every person shall be resurrected in the state he died.'
(Muslim)
Imagine you are enjoying this filthy film or soap with your mates and 'knock knock!' (No time to ask "who's there?") Its time to go! The Angel of Death has arrived. Think dear brothers and sisters who will be able to save us in front of humanity, our parents, our family and all the messengers when we shall be caught red handed or shall I say black handed if we had the remote control!
Can't happen? 3 years ago in the area of Lancashire a couple sat enjoying a movie over their tea. A hilarious joke came up and the wife burst into laughter, but noticed that she was the only one laughing. Looking across the room she saw her husband sitting there frozen, no longer alive to laugh or respond! A totally healthy fit young man suddenly dies! This happens time and again. The Arab proverb goes 'wise is he who takes a lesson from others'

Let us look at the statistics.

The following statistics have been extracted from the famous book;' The Devastating Effects of TV'

TV is one of the major causes of lethargy. (means you get tired and battered).

TV is responsible for the falling standards of literacy (no wonder they keep making the exams easier year after year huh!)

Takes one away from reality. (could say that again!)

TV has changed, and is still changing British life physically, culturally, socially and morally (I' m sure if there was another ally in the authors head he would have said it!)

90% of university students that are addicted to TV are immature; their level of communication being at the sixth grade level (sorry guys I never said that...)

It encourages an acceptance of aggression as a mode of behaviour.

A German social expert after personally conducting a thorough study of different schools and institutes, said with regards to the dangers of television on society and the new generation 'destroy the system of television before it destroys you...'

Ok I think that's enough! Although I've got a whole book in front of me bursting with facts and figures, for an intelligent man or woman a single sentence should be enough to change. May Allah grant us death (wait! Don't say 'Ameen,' look what I just wrote, let me finish!) in a state with which He shall be pleased with us, (now you can say it) Ameen! One final story to help us understand.

The Stranger

A few months before I was born, my dad met a stranger who was new to our small town. From the beginning, dad was fascinated with this enchanting newcomer, and soon invited him to live with our family. Though his outward appearance was not attractive, the stranger was quickly accepted and was around to welcome me into the world a few months later.

As I grew up I never questioned his place in our family. In my young mind, each member had a special place. My brother, Yusuf, a few years my senior, was my example. Sa'diyah, my younger sister, gave me an opportunity to play 'big brother' and develop the art of teasing. My parents were complementary instructors- Mum taught me to love Allah ta'ala and Dad taught me how to obey Him. But the stranger, who was our storyteller, could weave the most fascinating tales. Adventures, mysteries and comedies were daily conversations. He could hold our whole family spellbound for hours each evening and would take most of our time over the weekend. If I wanted to know about politics, history, or science, he knew it. He knew about the past and seemed to understand the present. The pictures he could draw were so life-like that I would often laugh or cry as I watched. He was like a friend to the whole family. He took dad, Yusuf and me to our first major league cricket game. He was always encouraging us to see the movies and he even made arrangements to introduce us to several famous people.

The stranger was a constant talker. Dad didn't seem to mind, but sometimes Mum would quietly get up- (while the rest of us were enthralled with one of his stories of a faraway place)- and go to her room and read the Qur'an. She would sometimes quietly tell us that the Holy Prophet Sallallahu Alayhi Wasallam said: 'the beauty of one's faith is shunning all non-productive activities.'

I wonder now if she ever prayed that the stranger would leave. Yes you see my dad ruled our household with certain moral convictions. But the stranger never felt an obligation to honour them. Swearing, for example, was not allowed in our house, neither from our friends, adults or us. Our long time visitor, however, used occasional four letter words that burned my ears and made dad squirm. To my knowledge the stranger was never confronted. My dad was a teetotaller who didn't permit alcohol in the house. But the stranger felt like we needed exposure and enlightened us to other ways of life. He offered us beer and other alcoholic beverages often. He made cigarettes look tasty, cigars manly and pipes distinguished. He talked freely about sex. His comments sometimes blatant, sometimes suggestive, and generally embarrassing. He showed us how to woo and flirt with women. I know now that my early concepts of the man-woman relationship were influenced by the stranger.

As I look back, I believe it was Allah's mercy that the stranger did not influence us more. Yet he was seldom rebuked and never asked to leave. More than thirty years have passed since the stranger moved in with the family. He is now not nearly so interesting to my dad as he was in those early years. But if I were to walk into my parents' bedroom today, you would still see him sitting over in a corner, waiting for someone to listen to him, talk and watch him draw his pictures and enchant his audience with his magic.

His name? You may ask... We call him T.V.

Sometimes we laugh, sometimes we cry, they say times have changed but its people who change. One minute someone's your best friend, you know no one better than him, the next minute he is your worst enemy. Every single limb in your body wants to hurt him. Why? What happened? Something he did or said changed everything (friendship problem).

Everything was going really well at school: Star pupil, top of the class in all the subjects, adored by every teacher. Then one day you happen to be in the wrong place at the wrong time... get blamed for something you never dreamt off... everything gone, whoever you pass by begins to whisper and point fingers at you, blamed, accused and reputation down the drain. (School problems).

You love going home from school to see and meet your mum and dad, you love them to bits and you would give your life for them, but you just feel so hurt when they begin to quarrel and it's a no win zone, each one is trying to shout the other out or it's a one way shout. You just sit in your room hoping they would understand each other, wishing they knew how you felt. Praying you could do something to help... (Family problems).

Everyone everywhere has problems. If life was as happy as we all wished it to be then this would no doubt be Jannah, but this is the world where things are different. One thing we should never forget is that whatever the problem, however severe it gets we are never alone and never will be, because Allah knows...

"Not a leaf falls except that He knows. There is not a grain in the darkness (or depths) of the earth, nor anything fresh or dry (green or withered), but it is inscribed in a clear book." (surah 6 verse 59)

Once a lady was doing tawaf of the kabah, singing some couplets: 'Oh Allah had You not given me the strength to bear all the difficulties that came crumbling onto me like a mountain I would have been no more. Oh Allah, I thank You for helping me throughout these hard times.'

Someone hearing her voice asked,

"What were those difficulties that you sing of?"

She said: "Oh be gone! I have never told anyone of my problems." The questioner persisted and the lady felt forced to narrate the following incident.

"It was the days of Eid ul Adha. My husband, having slaughtered a lamb for us had come inside to dine. One of my sons said to the other,

"Come let me show you how father cut the lamb." In doing so he accidentally killed his brother. Seeing what he had done, he ran off into the mountains. My husband went in search for him while I looked in shock at my dead son.

I waited for a long time but my husband did not return. I came out of the house to enquire and saw a man running down from the mountain. When he came close, he told me that my son was killed by a wolf and my husband, trying to save him, had fallen from the cliff. I was so star·lled to hear this news that I forgot I had left my 6 month old child in the house. Entering the home I saw he had crawled into the water pot and burnt his whole skin. He also died instantaneously. My sister, hearing the news, came and, when she saw my state screamed and died in shock. I was left alone with no one except my Allah. (Rowdhatu Rayyaheen)

When we're drowning in our problems, remember there's someone out there in a worse situation than us. Be patient: 'Verily, with every difficulty there is relief.' (Surah 94 Verse 6)

Dear sisters and brothers, at the end of the dark tunnel light awaits us. Patience and repentance. Look at the story of Yusuf (alayhi salam). A messenger of Allah, yet look how he is tested, in his early teens taken away from his father by his own flesh and blood, thrown into a well, sold as a slave, accused of something he never did, placed in jail for fourteen years..
Then light came, and he was made the king of Egypt. Subhanallah, united with his father after forty long years. (The Qur'an says this is the best story ever told.

Its got everything in it, romance, crime, betrayal etc.. give it a read if you get the chance.)

At the end of the story Yusuf (alayhi salam) says: "Verily my Lord understands best the mysteries of all that He plans to do. For verily, He is full of knowledge and wisdom." (Surah 12 Verse 100) It maybe Allah is planning something better for us. "It is possible that you dislike a thing which is good for you, and that you love a thing which is bad for you. But Allah knows and you know not." (Surah 2 Verse 216)

There was once a minister who was in the habit of always saying, 'Whatever has happened is good'. One day he went on a hunting trip with the king. Upon arriving at the destination, the king pulled out his bow & arrow and got pricked, which caused him to bleed. The minister immediately said 'Whatever has happened is good.

' The King became furious, saying " I am in pain and you say its good! Imprison him at once till I return!" As he was being taken away he uttered the same sentence:

'Whatever has happened is good.'

The king continued his hunt alone and soon he was deep into the jungle where he was cornered by cannibals. They carried him and took him to their master, where a ceremony was taking place and these cannibals were in search for a human to sacrifice. They placed the king on the slate ready for sacrifice and as he lay there trembling from head to toe the chief called out,

"Check the body, it must be free from any type of cuts and bruises!" When they checked the King's body out they saw that his finger was cut and so let him go. The king ran for his life, and upon arriving at the palace called for the minister immediately.

"I now understand the reality of your statement regarding me, but when I sent you away you said the same. What good was in that?" the minister explained "Well its obvious ain't it your Lordship? I never had a cut, so I would have become their meal."

Let us be strong and look on the bright side, whatever the problem may be. Some people due to excessive worrying become the victims of depression. Emotional changes happen to everyone. You know they say marriage is like the weather, but in reality one's entire life's like the weather. Believe it or not some of the greatest saints go through these sorts of phases called 'Qabdh' in which their heart and body don't feel like doing anything. So we're no exception.

Just look at the climate: sometimes it rains and rains like its never gonna stop and sometimes its so hot that the sun's rays feel doubled in strength. You've just got to keep going and bear everything that comes your way. Be firm on your feet just as a rock stands amidst the ever rising waves of the ocean.

This alternation of the day and night, happiness and sadness is a lesson for us all. The one who is drowning in the river of misery should know that the break of dawn is near. And the one who thinks he's got it all and is oppressing and troubling the creation of Allah beware the night is nigh...

Let us take heed from the following incident if we are causing anyone grief.

Once a couple sat to dine as the rain stormed against their window panes. Suddenly a knock came on the door. The wife ran to the door, wondering who it could be in such weather. As she opened the door she saw a beggar in rags sitting at the doorstep with his hands outstretched, saying:

"Please, for Allah's sake give me one boti (meat piece) and one roti (chapatti)." The wife was touched and went immediately to fetch some food. Her husband, already angry for being disturbed at his meal time, stood up and marched to the door. He looked down at the beggar, gave him one kick and slammed the door on his face...

The beggar took a sigh, looked up to the heavens and moved away.

Years went by and the rich man's business began to deteriorate. Slowly but surely he was close to bankruptcy and had to tell his wife to leave for he could no longer afford to keep her. Then, it so happened that he had to sell his house to pay his way through life. In spite of this his money soon expired and he was left with nothing except his own clothes, and forced onto the streets to beg.

He went from door to door knocking asking for some food to keep his back straight, but no one would give anything. Late one day, he arrived at a huge mansion. Hoping for something from this great home, he rapped at the door. Knock! knock! The lady in the house hurried towards the door and as she opened it, fell down unconscious with a scream. The husband came running to see who had troubled his dear beloved wife. Seeing a beggar at the door, he gave him lots of food from the house and some money. He also bade him farewell so that he could attend to his wife. When she regained conscious she said:

"Many years ago I sat to dine with my ex husband and someone similar came to the door. My husband treated him harshly and shooed him away. Now, the man that just came to our door was the very same ex husband who was so rich once upon a time. The new husband looked at his wife with love and said:

"Shall I tell you something more amazing? It was I , the

one who knocked on your door those many years ago as a beggar!"

Oh bullies and oppressors out there! Listen very carefully for Allah says in his glorious book;
"Do not think Allah to be ignorant of the deeds of those who do wrong. He is only giving respite till a day when the eyes shall be fixed in horror."
(surah 14 ayah 42)

Turn to Allah now and humble before you crumble!

For those that have been the victims of bullying and oppression, do not worry, for Allah is on your side. But let us be stronger than them and show them that we do not care, by forgiving them!
One sunny day two best friends went for a day at the beach. Their names were Ahmad and Yusuf. Ahmad said something to Yusuf which greatly angered him and caused him to slap Ahmad on the face. Ahmad immediately sat down and began to write on the sand:

Date: 12 Sept'
Today my best friend slapped me on my face.
(Ahmad.)

As they carried on they decided to have a little swim in the ocean. Ahmad was not a good swimmer and began to drown. Yusuf swam as fast as he could and brought him to shore. Ahmad immediately found a nail and began to engrave on a rock nearby:

Date: 12 Sept'
Today my best friend saved my life.
(Ahmad)

This time Yusuf was more composed to ask what was all this about, to which Ahmad said: "When you hurt me I

did not want to remember it so I wrote it on sand, for when the winds of forgiveness shall blow the effects of the slap can also be blown away. And when you saved my life it was something I wanted to remember so I wrote it on the rock, engraving the memory in my heart in a similar way."

So next time someone says something to us, just remember, write it on the sand...

Friends, if we do stumble and fall in life then please don't give up. Just like when a road is blocked we take the diversion and carry on, our diversion is du'a and tawbah (repentance) for Allah's mercy is ever-ready (no I don't mean the battery). He wants to take us back into his court and he sends a caller every night to ask "Is there anyone asking for forgiveness that I may forgive him? Is there anyone in need, so that I may help him?" You and I can do it! Shaytan only wants us to join him in the Hell fire.

I remember when I was really worried about something in life, my teacher wrote a lengthy letter consoling me and his last lines stuck in my head: 'With Faith and Fortitude all is Conquerable!'

End of school day

Girl 1: see ya.
Boy: Yeah you too.
Girl1: Take care, Gonna miss you. Cum on Msn ok! We'll
chat.
Boy: k.

Half an hour later...

www.msn.co.uk
Girl 1 :Hi you ok?
Boy: Yeah you? What you doing?
Girl 1: Nothing much.
Boy: I luv u
Girl 1: Me2

Suddenly an add pops up wanting to join
Allow?
Boy: Yes.
Hi ASL?
Boy: 16 M UK. You?
Girl 2: 16 F USA.

Previous screen pops up.

Girl 1: hey where do you go to?
Boy: O sos I'm busy ma old man s calling me catch you
later.

Girl 1: Oah!
Boy: Sos man gotta go.
Girl1: Okay. Xxx

Back on new screen.

Girl 2: You free?
Boy: Yeah you?
Girl2: Yep!
Boy: Got web cam?
Girl2: Yes sir.
Boy: Wanna see you. send ur pic.
Picture appears.
Boy: Wow. You look a beauty. Xxx
Girl 2: So do you wanna be friends?
Boy: more than friends!

To be continued.....

A new relationship has begun... or so he thinks (find out soon...) Ever come across stuff like that? Or is it all gobble-de-gook to you? Cyberspace! The World Wide Web has indeed spun the web across the globe catching millions of innocent people...
Stay online till we meet again... farewell... wassalam
Please send your comments, suggestions and questions to:
theworldof_teens@yahoo.com
Or if you don't wanna get caught in the web then write to
An Nasihah PO BOX 7737, LEICESTER, LE5 5XU, UK.

BIBLIOGRAPHY

The meaning of the Glorious Qur'an.
Abdullah Yusuf Ali.
Amana Publications.

Tambihul Ghafilin.
Abu Layth Samarqandi.
Darul Kutub Al Arabiya Beirut.

Mishkaat ul Masaabeeh.
Abu Muhammad Husayn ibn Masud Bagawi.
Qadimi Kutub Khana.

Zadul Talibeen.
Muhammad Ashiq Ilahi Al Barni.
Prudence Publications.

Misbahul Lugat.
Abu fadl Moulana Abdul Hafiz Balawi.
Darul Isha'at.

Music Exposed.
Siraj Ibn Yusuf Lambat
Time Publications.